Cheerleading Basics: Your Beginners Guide

ISBN-13: 978-1481112086
ISBN-10: 1481112082

Copyright Notice

CHEERLEADING BASICS: YOUR BEGINNERS GUIDE

Rebecca Lennison

For wannabe cheerleaders everywhere...

Contents

The History of Cheerleading

Cheerleading as an activity is said to have begun during the late 1880s in the United States. It started simply as the unified chanting, yelling, and clapping of a crowd in support of a sports team.

Although no one can say for sure how or why it is considered as such, the very first cheer was said to have been made by students of Princeton University in the year 1884.

They made a Princeton cheer and chanted it at a game, thus officially marking the birth of cheerleading.

A few years after that, the University of Minnesota was introduced to cheering by Tom Peebles, a graduate of Princeton.

And in November of 1898, a Minnesota student named Johnny Campbell directed what the world now knows as the very first organized cheer.

It is said that Minnesota was experiencing a terrible season in football at the time, such that their supporters felt they needed to create a chant that would motivate their team and bring positive results.

This stemmed from a thesis prepared by one of the students, which stated that fan support effectively sends positive energy towards the team, thus helping them win.

The Minnesota students gave their all when they cheered, but their team still lost the game. Nevertheless, what they did cemented the place of cheerleading in the world of sports.

It marked the beginning of organized cheers being seen at almost every sporting event.

The world's first male cheer squad was born in Minnesota in 1903 and this led to the organization of the world's first cheerleading fraternity as well, named Gamma Sigma.

Those who know cheerleading only as an activity where girls in shorts skirts are thrown into the air may be surprised to find out it actually began as an all-male activity.

The reason for this was that people then felt the deep male voice projects better than the shrill female voice.

Women only became more involved in cheerleading in the 1920s, when gymnastics, throws, and pyramids were first incorporated into the sport.

This was actually what elevated cheerleading to the level of a sport.

And in the 1930s, cheerleading team members came up with more entertaining routines, thus transforming the sport into a spectacular display of showmanship and skills.

In the 1900s, two major additions were introduced to the sport – the megaphone and pom-poms. Lawrence Herkimer, who introduced pom-poms to cheerleading, also founded the National Cheerleading Association and started the first cheerleading camps in 1946.

It is no wonder, then, that he is hailed as the grandfather of the sport.

Today, cheerleading is seen as a highly competitive sport that requires high levels of athleticism.

And while the sport is now made up of predominantly female cheerleaders, cheerleading routines usually display the incredible talents of both male and female members of a cheerleading squad.

The University of Minnesota and Lawrence Herkimer have indeed successfully expanded what Princeton University first introduced.

We have them to thank for one of the world's most exciting and fun sporting events to behold.

Benefits of Cheerleading

Cheerleading is one sport where the art of dance is combined with cheering talent and the skills of tumbling as well as executing jumps and stunts.

The activity itself has a unique way of drawing attention to a sporting event and encouraging audience participation and involvement.

Those who wish to become cheerleaders, of course, need to have natural talent and undergo proper training to develop the necessary skills and abilities.

The life of a cheerleader involves constant practice and dedication to the craft. And as you may have noticed, the one thing cheerleaders have in common is that they're all physical fit and in perfect shape.

It also helps for you to have enhanced flexibility if you wish to engage in cheerleading.

Of course, you'll have to be confident as well; otherwise, you aren't likely to survive in the world of cheerleading.

The value of constant practice lies in the need for you to master the fundamental hand movements, floor routines, and jumps.

You'll also have to keep working on your dancing skills, tumbling skills, and voice skills.

So, to become a cheerleader, you need natural talent, an energetic and bubbly personality, and the natural ability to make people smile and literally bring cheer to the occasion.

There are a number of benefits you can gain from cheerleading.

Perhaps the most notable benefit is that it increases your confidence, particularly when you perform under pressure in front of a large audience.

Cheerleading also provides you with a lot of opportunities to interact and bond with your peers. It can help develop a positive attitude towards life in general.

Cheerleaders naturally have the ability to lift each other up during bad times and celebrate the good times together. They are generally optimistic and constantly on the move.

Furthermore, the regular workout schedules required in cheerleading helps improve your strength, stamina, physical coordination, and overall fitness.

Take note that good physical conditioning and coordination can have positive effects on various aspects of your life.

Cheerleading also teaches you how to be a good team player and to trust the other people on your team.

Although cheerleading does involve a high risk for injury owing to the various manoeuvres and stunts you need to perform, it also involves a lot of excitement and fun.

Cheerleading is now seen at various sporting events such as football, basketball, and baseball.

And there are even separate competitions held exclusively for cheerleading.

The activity has indeed gone a long way since it was first developed to provide support to college football teams.

There are now a number of cheerleading institutions and camps that offer guidance and coaching to would-be cheerleaders.

There are also a lot of experienced cheerleaders who are willing to guide those who are new to the sport.

Men and women alike with a passion for the sport as well as the necessary physical attributes and skills can always become successful cheerleaders.

And you get to enjoy the various cheerleading benefits as you strive to continually improve your cheerleading skills.

The Dangers of Cheerleading

Cheerleading has long since been accepted as part of sporting events like football.

These days, however, it is widely accepted as a sport in itself.

And just like any other sport, it has its own set of dangers and risks.

Some of these risks result from poor coaching whereas others are a natural result of the structure of the sport.

After all, there's a lot more to cheerleading than dancing and chanting.

A perfect cheerleading routine involves perfectly choreographed gymnastics moves, perfectly executed somersaults and flips, and even being used as a human catapult.

When cheerleading is done on a floor area that's especially designed for the sport, then the risks are significantly reduced.

However, cheerleaders don't always perform on the ideal floor area.

Add to that the fact that cheerleading routines have become a lot more complex over the years and you'll understand how the risk for head, neck, and shoulder injuries is significantly increased.

It's amazing how unmindful cheerleaders can seem to be about the fact that they're risking their lives each time they perform.

To aggravate the risks involved in cheerleading, there are still schools that do not consider it a sport.

The activity therefore does not have the same strict safety regulations as other sports in many cases.

And a number of cheerleading coaches don't have certifications for training and safety. There are also schools that have a cheerleading squad, but don't really have the right equipment to ensure cheerleading safety.

Many cheerleading squads also practice on hardwood floors, which increases the risk for injury in case a cheerleader falls.

It's sad that this exciting sport has not been given due focus in terms of safety and minimizing the risks involved.

Medical records show that cheerleaders who have become permanently disabled have doubled in number and those who have suffered from serious injuries have grown more than triple in number.

Take note that any activity involving both motion and height is naturally very risky.

And only floors used in formal cheerleading competitions are really safe for cheerleaders because other surfaces such as basketball courts or football fields aren't built with cheerleading in mind.

Before you even start training to become a cheerleader, it's important for you to be fully aware of the dangers it poses so you can make a well-informed decision on whether this is indeed the right sport for you or not.

You need to be aware of the current lack of investment into the maintenance of safety in the sport so you can take the necessary precautions on your own.

Those precautions involve getting proper training and building a strong yet flexible physique that helps ensure you're able to perform the stunts and routines with the right form.

When you decide to take up cheerleading as a sport, you need to make sure the squad you join has a coach who's duly qualified and medically proficient, so you can be sure he knows what he is doing.

It would also be smart to try out for a cheerleading squad that invests in the safety of its cheerleaders.

Preventing Injuries

Don't ever think cheerleaders are immune from injury.

In fact, the risk for injury may be even greater in cheerleading than in other sports. Among the most common complaints associated with cheerleading are ankle and other muscle injuries.

Whenever you suffer from such injuries, it's understandable that your enjoyment of the entire cheerleading experience will be hampered.

That's why it's very important for you to do everything you possibly can to maintain an excellent physical condition.

Among the best ways for you to stay in good shape for cheerleading is to exercise regularly and do some stretches.

These activities not only help you avoid common cheerleading injuries, but also enhance your overall performance in the sport.

If you're just a beginner in the sport and are just starting to engage in a workout program, it's best for you to take it easy to begin with and then gradually work your way to more intense workouts as you grow stronger.

It is advisable to begin working out three times each week and then just add more days when you feel strong enough.

Bear in mind that over-training can be just as bad as a lack of training, which is why you need to find the proper balance in terms of cheerleading practice and workouts.

Another important thing you need to always bear in mind is the value of warming up before going through any workout or exercise routine.

Cardio exercises are often the best forms of warm-up activity.

You could run on the treadmill, jump rope, or perform any cardio exercise you find interesting.

What's important is that your heart rate is increased and your body is sufficiently warmed up.

Strengthening your upper body normally involves weight-lifting exercises. Among the best exercises for this purpose are arm curls, overhead presses, and bench presses.

If possible, perform a minimum of ten repetitions for each exercise in three sets. The first set of repetitions may be performed with a lighter weight and then graduate to heavier weights for the next two sets.

If you don't want to go to the gym and don't have weights at home, then you may strengthen your muscles by performing exercises that make use of your own body weight.

Push-ups and pull-ups are perhaps the best examples of these exercises.

For strengthening your legs, squats and lunges are the most commonly advised exercises. Just as you did with your upper body exercises, begin with three sets for each exercise. This time, though, it's best to strive for a minimum of 15 repetitions per set.

Always remember that the power you need for cheerleading jumps originate mainly from your legs, which is why leg strength is of utmost importance.

A good workout routine is something all cheerleaders should engage in on a regular basis.

The benefits of doing so aren't just limited to the prevention of common cheerleading injuries. It helps by providing you with more strength and agility for better cheerleading performance as well.

It is therefore important for you to incorporate a workout schedule into your cheerleading practice and training routine.

Developing Proper Posture

If you seriously want to become a cheerleader, then the first thing you need to do is get your back straight. Proper posture is essential to safe and effective cheerleading.

Of course, before you begin any exercise program that's meant to help you develop proper posture, it would be best for you to consult your doctor or personal fitness trainer.

After all, you need to make sure you can perform the necessary exercises without putting yourself at an unnecessary risk.

Another thing you need to make sure of is that you execute stretching exercises using the proper form and technique.

Performing posture-enhancing stretches and other forms of exercise without undergoing the proper training or using the right technique can increase your risk for injury.

Bear in mind as well that there's a different set of stretching exercises that's ideal for each person, so you'll have to find one that's just right for you.

Although it can be easy to understand why good posture is important for activities like cheerleading, developing the right posture is often easier said than done.

And for most people, a huge part of their daily routines actually prevent them from adopting good posture.

The good news for you is that there are a number of simple exercises that can help improve your posture and prepare you for cheerleading.

You can incorporate these exercises into the exercise or workout routine you're currently following.

As a result of incorporating posture-enhancing stretches into your workout routine, you can expect to get an improved level of flexibility, recover more quickly from your workouts, and keep away from common injuries when cheerleading season finally arrives.

These are just some of the benefits stretching exercises have to offer. Other important benefits include a significant reduction in instances of back pain, improved blood circulation, and better oxygen uptake.

A stress fracture suffered by your lumbar vertebrae is said to be the most commonly experienced back injury by teenagers.

Even more telling is the fact that gymnasts and cheerleaders are the ones most commonly affected by the injury, primarily because their sport of choice demands a great deal more flexibility than most of the other types of sports.

Other than the nature of their sport, this common problem among cheerleaders can also be attributed to tight muscles resulting from jumping and tumbling, weak core muscles, and constant hyper extension of your back muscles during stunts, among other factors.

Experts suggest that the best way to prevent such injury is to promote proper posture through strengthening your core muscles.

To be more specific, you can improve your flexibility by strengthening your abs as well as your abdominal wall.

Additionally, this also helps improve your circulation and lessen recovery time in case of an injury.

It is also advised for you to incorporate stretches into both your warm-up and cool-down routines every time you work out.

This allows you to keep your muscles healthy and limber, while helping improve your overall fitness level at the same time.

Improving Core Strength

If you're currently in the process of developing a workout routine in hopes of improving your overall performance in cheerleading, then you need to make sure that your core strength is taken into account.

Enhancing your core strength allows you to execute the various cheerleading moves more easily and helps keep you safe from the common injuries associated with cheerleading.

Furthermore, core strengthening exercises also help you develop more stability, which helps ensure that you always stay on your feet whenever you land from any of your cheerleading jumps and then immediately move on to your next movement.

People with a weak core will normally find this very difficult to do, and such difficulty naturally hinders their overall performance. Here are some of the exercises that can help you improve core strength:

1. Plank with Exercise Ball

The first core strengthening exercise on the list is ideal for developing not just muscle strength, but endurance as well.

The simple plank exercise already helps you achieve this goal, but you can increase its intensity by placing your hands on an exercise ball while doing the plank.

Take note that this is a more advanced exercise and should be done only when you've reached the point of being able to hold a standard plank for more than 30 seconds.

If you go for the exercise ball plank right away, you may have problems trying to maintain stability.

2. Decline Sit-ups with a Twist

The mere fact that you'll be forced by this exercise to work against gravity already assures you of its intensity. What's good about this exercise is that it works the muscles that line your stomach along with your oblique muscles.

This makes it a truly ideal core-strengthening exercise overall. It is best to perform this exercise using slow and controlled movements so as to maintain as much tension on your muscles as possible throughout the length of the exercise.

3. The Bicycle

This is another excellent exercise to include in your cheerleading workout routine. It will effectively work your oblique muscles and your front core muscles at the same time.

Other than that, this exercise is also very effective for helping you maintain control over your body, which is obviously very important when you're trying to execute advanced cheerleading movements and routines. When you perform the bicycle exercise, remember to keep your feet elevated so as to maintain tension in your lower abs.

These are just three of the best exercises you can perform regularly in order to strengthen your core. It is essential that you incorporate them into your regular cheerleading workout routine.

Experts advise that you need to do at least three sets during each workout session for at least twice each week to begin with.

These core-strengthening exercises will surely get you started on the way to cheerleading success.

Bear in mind that a strong core will not only help you ensure success as a cheerleader; it'll help you ensure your safety at all times as well.

Improving Flexibility

One of the things you need to focus on when you're working to become a cheerleader is improving your flexibility.

Not only does flexibility enable you to perform those amazing splits and stunts, but it also helps you stay away from muscle injuries.

This is why stretching needs to be a mainstay of your workout routine for cheerleading.

And you should take note that it's not just the type and amount of stretching you do that's important; *when* you do perform stretching exercises is important as well.

Some people generally advise you to stretch before starting your workout. There are also those who swear by stretching after a workout session.

But, what experts most commonly advise is for you to do your stretches after your warm-up session. This is when you'll gain the most number of benefits from the stretching exercises you do.

Splits are perhaps the one movement that require you to do stretches more than any other movement.

The good news is that there are plenty of stretching exercises you can perform to improve on your ability to do splits.

What's important is for you to bear in mind that you shouldn't bounce when stretching. Instead, you need to hold each stretching position for about 30 seconds before moving on to the next.

When you're just beginning to work out for cheerleading, you'll likely be able to hold a position for only ten seconds. That's just fine.

You just have to gradually increase the intensity of the stretch and the time you hold the position as your strength and flexibility increases. This helps ensure that you continue to improve.

As you go through your routine, be sure to breathe naturally and stretch in a relaxed manner.

A lot of beginners make the mistake of holding their breath on a stretch. Be sure to avoid this mistake.

One of the best stretches you can perform for cheerleading purposes is the Standing Hamstring. This is performed by placing one of your feet on a chair and bending your knee. Curve your back inward as you lean forward.

Take note that the stretch should be felt in the hamstring of the leg that's on the chair. Hold the position for 10-30 seconds (depending on your current level of flexibility) and then repeat the movement with the other leg.

Another excellent stretching exercise is done by sitting on the floor and holding your legs straight out front.

Bend forward slowly and strive to touch your toes.

Hold the position for 10-30 seconds. If you are unable to reach your toes the first time, just try to reach forward as far as you can go.

Be sure to try reaching farther forward each time you perform this stretch and bear in mind that the ultimate goal is to reach your toes and get your nose to touch your knees.

These are just two of the stretches you can do to effectively improve your flexibility for purposes of cheerleading.

You'd do well to research other stretches that work just as well and use them to your advantage.

Improving Endurance

Most cheerleaders focus on strength and flexibility when they train for cheerleading.

What you may not realize is that the short yet consistent periods of intense aerobic activity requires endurance as well.

The fast-paced cheerleading routines require the ability to maintain a high level of strength and flexibility all throughout the period covered by the routine. This is why you need to build muscle endurance as well.

Running is often thought to be the best form of exercise for building endurance. It is indeed an excellent form of exercise, but you may want to try other exercises as well to keep your routines fun and exciting.

One exercise you may want to try is jumping rope. This is ideal for when you don't really have much time for your workout.

Jumping rope at high speeds can effectively raise your heart rate and provide you with a good workout in just a short period of time.

If running is really your exercise of choice, then you'd do well to warm up with a slow and short run. After that, you can move on to short sprints in order to build endurance.

When you sprint, you have the option of determining a specific distance, sprinting for that distance, jogging back to the starting point, and then repeating the movement.

If your chosen distance is relatively short, then you can choose to walk back to starting point. If you choose to sprint around a track, then you have the option of sprinting halfway down the track and then jogging for the rest of the way.

Whatever you choose to do for building endurance, it's important that you find an activity that you really like. This helps ensure that you're always motivated and even excited to do your workouts.

Doing something you love to do makes exercising a lot more fun. You could try a variety of cardiovascular exercises until you find the activity you enjoy most.

You can even increase the fun by exercising to your favourite music or exercising with a group of friends. Not only does this allow you to enjoy a good workout, but it also helps you catch up on the latest news from your friends.

To make sure your exercises continually help you improve, it's best to start out slow and then gradually build up the intensity and pace. Be careful not to force yourself to do too much at once, as that will only lead to injury.

You should also remember to warm-up before your exercise session and cool down afterwards in order to gain the full benefits of your workout.

To keep from getting bored, it's also a good idea to alternate among a number of cardiovascular activities. For many people, variety is actually the key to a successful workout.

These are just a few of the ways you can build your endurance for cheerleading. You can vary your exercises and be as creative as you want.

What's important is that you get your heart rate up and try to do exercises in just a short period of time so you can stay away from marathon workouts.

After all, you don't want your workouts to take too much time away from your other important tasks, do you?

Improving Your Jump

Jumps are mainstays of cheerleading routines. If you're training to become a cheerleader, then this is something you definitely can't do without.

You'll have to learn and master cheerleading jumps as early in your training as possible.

Learning the proper jumping technique and constant practice are the most important things you can do to make your cheerleading performance a lot more impressive.

Don't be discouraged if you're unable to jump too high at first.

Instead, you should use that as a motivation to keep working until you achieve an excellent vertical jump.

One of the first things you need to bear in mind is that improving cheerleading jumps requires dedication.

This means you need to commit yourself to regular practice, enhancing your flexibility, and increasing your strength until you get your jumps just right.

Stretching exercises can do much to help you develop your jumping skills. It increases your range of motion and reduces soreness as well as the risk for injury.

Simply by stretching for 30 minutes each day, you can improve your performance of such cheerleading stunts as the splits.

Don't just perform standard stretching exercises. Be creative and try to think of other ways you can stretch such that actual cheerleading jumps and stunts are simulated.

And you don't even have to do the stretches for a straight 30 minutes. You can break the exercises up to manageable increments if you feel more comfortable that way.

You can also make stretching more fun by doing it with your favourite music or while watching TV. The good thing about stretching exercises is that you notice significant improvements within just a few weeks.

Bear in mind as well that there are several muscles used when performing cheerleading jumps.

When you lift your legs as you perform such stunts as toe touches, you use your hip flexors, for one thing.

It's also important for you to keep your thigh muscles strong, as that is needed for launching yourself off the ground. Among the best exercises for this purpose are squats and lunges.

Of course, exercises that involve jumping are advisable as well. Just remember to always apply the proper technique when you performing jumping exercises.

Other than your hip flexors and thighs, you should also work on your calf muscles. They may not be used that much for cheerleading jumps, but you can still gain a lot of benefits from strengthening your calf muscles. Simple exercises such as toe raises should do the trick.

This is done by standing on a platform with your heels positioned over the edge.

Start by lowering your heels and then lifting yourself up as high as you can.

Repeat the movement as many times as you can.

Once you've achieved enough strength and flexibility to improve the height of your jumps, you'll have to work on improving your technique.

Adopting the right posture as you jump is also very important in ensuring beautiful cheerleading jumps.

And always remember that determination and dedication are the keys to successfully improving your jumps in cheerleading.

Enhancing Your
Dancing Skills

Becoming a cheerleader involve not just jumps and stunts. To become good at what you do, you'll have to hone your dancing skills as well.

Towards this end, you'd do well to engage in some dance workouts whenever you spend time at the gym. These workouts help increase your strength as well as your muscle tone and leanness. As a result, you get to burn fat more quickly and maintain the perfect physique for cheerleading.

If you're like most people who are just beginning to train for cheerleading, then you'd probably hesitate to use weights when you exercise, thinking they'd cause you to grow big and bulky muscles.

On the contrary, moderate weights can actually help you achieve the kind of muscle tone and physique you're striving for. Here are some of the best exercises that can help enhance your dancing skills for cheerleading:

1. Step-ups

This is an excellent exercise for strengthening your lower body. It works on your quads to a large extent and targets your glutes as well.

Begin the exercise by holding a barbell across your back.

This should increase your strength gains from the exercise and considerably improve your balance as well. That's because the barbell will increase the resistance of the step-up movement.

2. Push-ups

This is also a very important exercise that can help increase your strength for a more explosive performance in dancing. It effectively targets just about every muscle in your upper body, thus helping strengthen your muscles even without using weights.

Try to execute full push-ups and keep your body properly aligned with each movement.

3. Single-leg Split Squats

Just like step-ups, this is also an excellent exercise for your lower body. It enhances the strength of your glutes, which is very important for such movements as cheerleading jumps.

In executing this exercise, try to drive yourself up through your glutes, since this is the area where your power should be generated. Lean backwards a little when doing this exercise and imagine yourself pressing up through your heels.

4. Mountain Climbers

This could be the perfect exercise to complete your dance workout. It effectively enhances your anaerobic capacity and improves your overall strength as well. That's because the exercise uses both your lower and upper body muscles.

When you perform this exercise, strive to jump your legs into your body as high up as you can. That really works your core muscles.

You should then kick your legs backward until they're fully extended such that maximum stress is placed on your upper body.

Try to complete three sets with 20 repetitions per set.

Incorporating these exercises into your dance workouts will surely enhance your dancing skills and help you become the best cheerleader that you can be.

They help develop your strength and flexibility, thus allowing you to perform more attractive and explosive dance moves.

Remember that not all cheerleaders can become flyers, which is why improving your dancing skills is one of the most important things you can do to gain entry into your chosen cheerleading team.

How Plyometrics Can Help

You may or may not know it, but plyometrics can actually help a lot if you want to become a successful cheerleader.

Among other things, it helps increase your speed, force, power, and ability to execute rapid movements. A lot of the movements you see in gymnastics are categorized as plyometric movements.

Needless to say, enhanced speed, force, and power are very useful in cheerleading.

Plyometric exercises are an excellent addition to your cheerleading workout routine. They allow you to benefit fully from each contraction of your muscles.

As a result, you'll be able to jump much higher and move much faster, which are indeed very useful in the sport of cheerleading.

Cheerleading routines are never complete without its myriad jumps and stunts. You'll be glad to know that plyometrics allows you to get more force and power behind your jumps.

This improves your overall performance and gets you prepared for competitive cheerleading.

How exactly do you incorporate plyometrics into your workout routine?

Well, adding any form of exercise that involves explosive movement should do the trick.

Jumping squats are an excellent example of effective plyometric exercises.

To perform this particular exercise, you need to carry a pair of dumbbells in your hands. Squat down and then explode into a jump as powerfully and quickly as you can. Repeat the movement for a specified number of repetitions and sets.

The weighted medicine ball is also a very useful tool when performing plyometric exercises.

Choose a blank wall in the gym and then get a medicine ball with a weight you can comfortably carry. Throw the ball up against the wall at the highest possible level.

Be sure to catch the ball as it comes back down and then immediately press up and throw the ball right back up against the wall.

Again, repeat for a specified number of repetitions and sets. This particular exercise can do wonders for the muscles of your upper body.

Another excellent plyometric exercise you should incorporate in your workout routine is the classic push-up.

Begin the exercise by going down on your knees and then dropping your upper body forward.

Catch your weight by placing your palms on the floor.

Drop as far down as you can and then explode back up until you're in an upright position on your knees.

Repeat the movement for a pre-determined number of repetitions and do at least three sets of the exercise to get the best results.

These are just some of the plyometric exercises you can choose to include in your cheerleading workout routine.

There are other exercises you can choose from that are equally effective and may even be a lot of fun.

Whatever form of plyometrics you choose to engage in, one thing's for sure: They'll help you attain the kind of cheerleading skills you want to have.

Your movements will become more precise and explosive.

You'll finally be able to move with purpose and this enhanced ability will definitely show in every cheerleading competition your team participates in.

Preparing for Cheerleading Tryouts

If you really want to become a cheerleader, then of course you need to try out for a cheerleading team. Doing so can be a very exciting yet scary experience, especially if you've never tried out before.

Perhaps the most important thing is for you to be sufficiently prepared before you even set foot on the tryout venue. Read on for some valuable tips on how to prepare for cheerleading tryouts.

The first thing you need to do is determine the requirements of the cheerleading squad you plan to join. Most cheerleading teams require at least the most basic tumbling skills. You may have to be proficient at performing round-offs and cartwheel, among other movements.

There are also squads that require more advanced skills like back tucks and handsprings. If you're looking to join a school cheerleading squad, then there may even be a required minimum grade point average.

In most cases, you'll also be required to have sufficient knowledge and skills in the basic cheerleading movements as well as the ability to come up with fund-raising and cheering events.

It may be a good idea to ask the team's coach or director so you'll know exactly what is required. You may even get some tips before tryouts begin.

As soon as you know exactly what the requirements are, you need to start working on your cheerleading skills right away.

A lot of the things you'll need to learn and develop will need a good deal of time so the earlier you start working on them, the better.

Even something as simple as a split can take months to master if you're a beginner without any previous cheerleading experience.

You'd do well to do some research on the exercises that may help you learn these skills more quickly and improve your overall cheerleading performance.

One of the best ways for you to prepare for cheerleading tryouts is to improve your flexibility. This is especially true if you're completely new to the sport. It is recommended that you stretch for at least 20 minutes each day to begin with.

The good news is that there are plenty of stretching exercises that can help you achieve your goal, so you can keep your routines fresh.

Tumbling is also an important skill to master when you're working to become a cheerleader. It's important for you to learn and master one form of tumbling at a time. Among the things you need to watch out for when you start learning tumbling are your body alignment and hand placement.

Take note that your body should always be in a straight line when you perform tumbling movements.

The cartwheel is a good place for you to start. You may want to record your practice on video so you'll see what you're doing wrong and how you can improve.

When tryout day finally arrives, you'll have to show the squad that you've already mastered the skills that they require.

Naturally, you'll have to do a cheer in front of the selection panel. Be sure to cheer from your diaphragm so you don't get a sore throat from screaming.

And don't forget to polish your dancing skills, as you'll likely be asked to memorize a dance routine a week prior to the schedule and perform the routine with other cheerleader wannabes on tryout day.

Tips for Tryout Day

As cheerleading tryout day approaches, it's important for you to know exactly how you should act and look.

On the night before tryout day, you need to get plenty of beauty sleep. Take note that your concentration and focus can be negatively affected by staying out late.

You should also make sure that you eat a healthy diet rich in proteins, vegetables, and fruits from the time you start preparing for the tryouts.

If you were a little overweight to begin with, don't get into a crash diet in hopes of losing excess weight. That will only result in you becoming lethargic and lacking the energy a cheerleader is expected to have.

Your practice and workout sessions, coupled with a healthy diet, should effectively get you to your ideal weight when tryout day finally arrives.

On the day of the tryout itself, be sure to look your best. Lift your hair up into a clean ponytail or pin it securely into a bun.

If you have short hair that can't be secured in a bun or tied into a ponytail, then you'd do well to pull it back with an elastic headband. Make sure the headband you use won't fall off as you perform your routine.

It may be an even better idea to wear a headband or ribbon in the squad's colors to show that you're serious about wanting to become part of the team.

Another important consideration for cheerleading tryouts is your outfit. Make sure the clothes you wear on tryout day are easy to move in and have a perfect fit.

Stay away from oversized t-shirts and baggy pants, as these can obstruct the tryout panel's view of your cheerleading moves.

A fitted t-shirt and a pair of practice shorts may be a better choice. It may also be smart to wear a Lycra cheer skirt so you'll really look the part of a cheerleader.

As regards your footwear, the best choice may be a pair of lightweight tennis shoes, as they offer the necessary support. There are also shoes made especially for cheerleading.

Bear in mind that cheerleading tryouts isn't the right venue for you to focus on style and glamour.

In fact, you need to stay away from too much makeup, glitters, jewelry, and extra-long fingernails when you're trying out for a cheerleading squad.

Avoid tryout injuries by warming up adequately a few minutes before tryouts begin.

And while it's understandable for you to be a little nervous, be sure to exude a confident attitude as you walk through the door and face the panel.

Of course, you'll have to exude enthusiasm and cheer as well.

After all, that's what being a cheerleader is about, right?

Be sure to speak clearly and in a voice that's loud enough for everyone in the venue to hear.

Even if you make a mistake in the routine, keep smiling and go on as if nothing out of the ordinary happened.

Most of the time, the tryout panel isn't looking for perfection, but for the right attitude.

While these tips may not really guarantee you a spot on your chosen cheerleading squad, it can certainly do much to increase your chances of getting in.

What's important is for you to do your best and be proud of what you've got to show.

Nutrition

When you decide to get into cheerleading, you'll have to take your nutrition into serious consideration, just as you would when getting into any other kind of sport.

Making sure that you eat a healthy diet will help ensure that you have enough energy for the movements required by the sport.

Proper nutrition also helps you build muscle strength and endurance, thus helping improve your overall cheerleading performance.

It is in cases such as this that you can truly appreciate what the saying, "you are what you eat" means. Consuming unhealthy foods will likely make you feel sluggish and inhibit muscle growth.

A healthy diet, of course, means eating the right kinds of food in the right amounts. This means you have to avoid fad diets or crash diets. Bear in mind as well that being on a healthy diet doesn't mean starving yourself.

Furthermore, you should avoid trying to lose excess poundage very quickly, as that only leads to unhealthy dieting.

Take note that unhealthy dieting accomplishes nothing except cheating yourself of the kind of nutrition you truly need and deserve.

A properly balanced diet allows you to achieve and maintain your ideal weight, while looking good at the same time.

Naturally, you understand how important it is for cheerleaders to always look their best.

Your body naturally needs a sufficient amount of proteins, carbohydrates, and healthy fats.

As you probably already know, proteins are your muscles' building blocks so you'll definitely need them for enhancing muscle strength and endurance.

Carbohydrates serve as your body's primary energy source and there is perhaps no need to explain why a cheerleader requires a great deal of energy.

And while fats are often labelled as the bad guy in nutrition, there are actually fats that are considered healthy and your body needs them in just the right amounts to maintain the health of your hormones and nervous system.

Make sure you consume these nutrients in the proper ratio with each meal, as they are the keys to an enhanced cheerleading performance. Experts usually recommend a diet that's high in carbohydrates with a moderate amount of protein and a little bit of fat.

Before you start a workout or practice session, it's a good idea to eat a meal that's rich in carbohydrates.

Your body has a natural tendency to digest carbohydrates a lot quicker and deliver glucose more quickly to your muscles.

Avoid consuming such foods as hamburgers, pizza, candy, and soda as well as dairy products before your workouts.

Remember as well to eat an hour to four hours before your workout or practice begins so your body has enough time to digest your food and process the nutrients it needs for fuel.

Whether you're engaged in cheerleading or any other sport, or even if you're not engaged in any sport at all, it's definitely important for you to ensure proper nutrition.

Not only does it keep your energy levels up, but it helps you maintain your overall health as well. And that's definitely something no amount of money can buy.

Benefitting from Cheerleading Camp

Cheerleading camp can offer you a great experience, whether you're a beginner in the sport or an experienced cheerleader.

It is the perfect venue for you to learn new cheers and stunts while improving your cheerleading skills and developing team-building skills at the same time.

Remember that cheerleading camp is naturally a busy time for you and you'll need to get as much from the experience as you can. Below are some tips on how you can fully benefit from cheerleading camp.

The first thing you need to do is choose the right camp for you and other members of your team.

Of course, cheerleading camp will be a lot more fun if you have your entire squad with you. But, that can only be true if you've made sure the camp you chose is the right one for your team.

You'll have to consider a number of things when deciding which particular camp to join. Among these things are your squad's financial resources, skill level, and goals for the coming cheerleading season.

Now, you may be wondering just what advantages a cheerleading camp has to offer.

Well, for one thing, it gives your squad's new members the chance to bond with the rest of the team in an environment of fun.

It also gives the entire team an opportunity to learn new cheers and skills while improving on the old ones.

Furthermore, you get to learn additional safety tips and training in cheerleading camp, particularly where tumbling and executing stunts are concerned.

You can also expect to enhance the team's teamwork and develop mutual trust among the members as a result of cheerleading camp.

Of course, just like anything else in this world, there are also some disadvantages to joining cheerleading camp. Perhaps the most notable disadvantage is the fact that cheerleading camp tends to be very costly.

Some of your squad members may not be able to afford camp so if you really want to get everyone to join, then you'll have to find ways of coming up with the necessary funds.

Most camps are also very competitive, which can be a boon to more experienced teams, but may not really be of help to new teams. Take note as well that your squad will have to be in top shape before attending camp.

If you do decide to take advantage of cheerleading camp, be sure to pay attention and listen carefully to what's being said because you're likely to be bombarded with information.

It's a good idea to take notes so you can review whatever was said at a later time. Should anything be unclear to you, never hesitate to ask questions.

In case you receive criticism, don't be discouraged and don't take it personally.

Criticisms are a normal part of cheerleading camp and you should use it to improve your craft. Participate as much as you can in competitions that are held as part of the camp.

If nothing else, you can at least get to practice performing to a critical audience.

Cheerleading camp is an excellent chance for your team to work together towards the same goal, which is the key to being a successful team.

Printed in Great Britain
by Amazon